Completing an Employment Application

Have You Ever Been Convicted of a Felony? Workbook

Shannon Ben Dailey

Completing an Employment Application

ISBN-13: 978-1985169807

Printed in the United States of America.

www.LiveDailey.com

CONTENTS

Disclaimer

All opinions expressed by the author in this book are solely the author's opinions and do not reflect the opinions of companies he has worked for and/or consulted with in the past or presently works for or consults with. All suggestions and opinions mentioned are not guaranteed to work. Each suggestion and opinion in this book that may have been advised, applied, and implemented may produce different results based on your past convictions and work history. The author's opinions are based upon information he considers reliable, useful, and resourceful. Neither the companies mentioned nor the companies the author worked for in the past, presently works for, and/or consulted with or consults with, along with any affiliates and/or subsidiaries, warrant this book's completeness or accuracy, and it should not be relied upon as such. The author and/or his affiliates and/or subsidiaries are not under any obligation to update or correct any information provided in this book.

Introduction

My name is Shannon Dailey, and I am an African-American male and a former convicted felon, born and raised in Cleveland, Ohio. I wrote *Dirt Road to Smooth Pavement*, which outlines my double conviction for drug trafficking and a weapons charge. I tell the story of how my life changed dramatically from making poor choices in my teen years as a drug dealer, with a limited work history, to leaving the street behind. I also wrote *Have You Ever Been Convicted of a Felony?*, which shares my experience as a former convicted felon to getting hired full-time with fortune 500 companies. I went from temp jobs to permanent positions to getting hired directly into management, a vice president of sales and marketing, to owning my own business to doing what I am ultimately passionate about—helping others like me succeed.

Getting Started

First off, thank you so much for making time to take advantage of this workbook. This workbook is designed to unpack tips, suggestions, and best practices from books that I wrote. This workbook goes hand in hand with *Have You Ever Been Convicted of a Felony?* Throughout this workbook, there will be references made to that book specifically; and in order to maximize the value of this workbook, it is highly recommended that you read *Have You Ever Been Convicted of a Felony?*

In the chapter "Completing an Employment Application" from *Have You Ever Been Convicted of a Felony?*, you should use what color of ink pen?

Also, before you continue utilizing this workbook, be sure to have a copy of your resume, along with a printout of your previous employers' information and references and achievements handy. You're going to need it.

Practice does not make you perfect, but it will increase your confidence, and that is exactly what this workbook is created to do—build confidence.

Personal Information

Here's your chance to practice completing your very own employment application. The chapter "Completing an Employment Application" from *Have You Ever Been Convicted of a Felony?* describes how to do just that. Please take a moment to review that chapter, and when ready, fill in the following. Try to be as accurate as possible using the proper color ink. Treat this workbook like an actual employment application.

In the chapter "The Big Question" from *Have You Ever Been Convicted of a Felony?*, depending on the state you live in and/or the company you are applying to work for, the question, "Have you been convicted of a felony or crime?" may not exist. In case the question does exist like on the application in this workbook, there are several examples used to describe various felony convictions. Take a moment to write your former conviction in below. Please refer to the chapter "The Big Question" for tips to assist you with how to explain your former conviction. Oh, and remember, nothing lengthy and keep it simple.

Please fill in the following:

Application For Employment

Personal Information

Name

Address	City	State

Phone Number	Mobile Number	Email Address

Are You A U.S. Citizen?	Have You Ever Been Convicted Of A Felony?
Yes ☐ No ☐	Yes ☐ No ☐

If you have been convicted, please explain

_____

_____

_____

Notes:

Position

The chapter "Hustling Mentality" from *Have You Ever Been Convicted of a Felony?* talks about how you should not apply for just any job. Under the section "Position You Are Applying or" listed below, you should never, ever write: ANY, WHATEVER IS AVAILABLE, or LEAVE IT BLANK. Can you honestly say that you would take absolutely any position? And if you are still thinking in your head, *Yes, I would take any job*, or you are tempted to write ANY or WHATEVER IS AVAILABLE in this section, please re-read chapter "Know Thyself" from *Have You Ever Been Convicted of a Felony?*

Please fill in the following:

Position	
Position You Are Applying For	Available Start Date

Employment Desired

☐ Full Time   ☐ Part Time   ☐ Seasonal/Temporary

Depending on the employment application that you have in front of you, that application may include a section to list the days you can or cannot work, along with which shifts you are available to work. Note of caution, do not say you are available seven days each week and can work any shift if you really can't. If you are available Monday through Saturday and can work first shift, then note that.

Selecting that you can work seven days each week and are available any shift just to get the job may not end well when they confirm your schedule in the interview.

Notes:

_____

_____

_____

_____

_____

_____

_____

_____

_____

Education

In the education section, start with your most recent college, schooling, or seminar training where you received a degree, license, or certification. If you only have a GED or high school diploma, then list it. Some employment applications may have a section for you to list training or skills. If there is not a section to list your training or skills, like this application, feel free to list your training or skills under the education section. Training or skills can be a number of things, such as being certified to operate a tow motor, being certified for data processing, having a sales license to sell cars, and so forth. Even if your training and skills are unrelated to the position that you are applying for, list them anyway.

Please fill in the following:

Education			
School Name	Location	Years Attended	Degree Received

Notes:

References

In the references section, this portion of the application is asking you to list three people you have worked with or worked under that will vouch for you. The people you list as a reference should be individuals that will speak well of your work productivity and character.

Some employment applications may request that you list general references, which could be an employee, family member, friend, or someone else that will speak well of your character or determination and willingness to work.

Please fill in the following:

References		
Name	Title	Company

Notes:

Employment History

In this final section of this employment application, please list the most recent company you worked for first and then work backward. Be sure to complete as much information as possible. If you only worked one job prior to completing this section, then list only the one job. If you worked for ABC Company as a temporary employee through AAA Staffing, then I suggest you list on the line for employer: ABC Company/AAA Staffing. Some applications may ask for a starting date and an ending date, or starting pay and ending pay. Even though you should know when you started and how much you made per hour, if you do not recall the exact start date with your previous employer, please do not leave it blank. If need be, write in your best educated guess. Try to be accurate as possible if you are not able to find out starting dates with prior employers.

Lastly, make sure you sign and date the employment application; and before you turn in the application, be sure to review it. Make sure it is error free and complete.

Please fill in the following:

Employment History

Employer (1)	Job Title	
Work Phone	Starting Pay Rate	
Address	City	State
Employer (2)	Job Title	
Work Phone	Starting Pay Rate	
Address	City	State
Employer (3)	Job Title	
Work Phone	Starting Pay Rate	
Address	City	State

Signature Disclaimer

I certify that my answers are true and complete to the best of my knowledge.
If this application leads to employment, I understand that false or misleading information in my application or interview may result in my release.

Name (Please Print)	Signature
Date	

Notes:

Practice Application

Now that you have completed all the sections of the employment application, let's do it again! On the following page, take your time completing the employment application. Remember, you are completing an application, not a test; you are not timed. Relax. Take your time to accurately fill in your employment application. When you complete it, double check your work for errors. If you need to make any corrections, simply line through the error or typo. DO not scribble over or black out the error. Lining through an error does not look as obvious as scribbles.

Once again, when you are done completing this application or any employment application, please take a moment to go over it. Check your own application as if you are recruiting yourself. Make sure you filled everything in to the best of your ability. Taking that extra 60 seconds or so to look over your application may be all the difference between getting hired or not.

Application For Employment

Personal Information

Name

Address		City	State

Phone Number	Mobile Number	Email Address

Are You A U.S. Citizen?

Yes ☐   No ☐

Have You Ever Been Convicted Of A Felony?

Yes ☐   No ☐

If you have been convicted, please explain

_____

_____

_____

Position

Position You Are Applying For	Available Start Date

Employment Desired

☐ Full Time   ☐ Part Time   ☐ Seasonal/Temporary

Education

School Name	Location	Years Attended	Degree Received

References

Name	Title	Company

28

Employment History

Employer (1)	Job Title	
Work Phone	Starting Pay Rate	
Address	City	State
Employer (2)	Job Title	
Work Phone	Starting Pay Rate	
Address	City	State
Employer (3)	Job Title	
Work Phone	Starting Pay Rate	
Address	City	State

Signature Disclaimer

I certify that my answers are true and complete to the best of my knowledge.
If this application leads to employment, I understand that false or misleading information in my application or interview may result in my release.

Name (Please Print)	Signature
Date	

www.LiveDailey.com

www.ingramcontent.com/pod-product-compliance
Lightning Source LLC
Chambersburg PA
CBHW081624220526
45468CB00010B/3016